Mentored Succession

A Smarter Way for Pastoral Transitions

by

Gene Roncone

©2022 by Gene Roncone. All rights reserved. No part of this book may be reproduced or used in any form without written permission from the author.

ABOUT THE AUTHOR

Gene Roncone is passionate about helping churches survive and thrive in pastoral leadership transitions. He presently leads the Rocky Mountain Ministry Network, providing support, resourcing, and training for over 160 churches and 500 ministers serving over 44,000 constituents in Colorado and Utah. Gene has authored several books that have been on Amazon's best-selling list for Christian clergy, including *Defying Gravity, Rise Up, Spirit-Friendly Leadership, Ministerial Ethics, Chairing Church Board Meetings, The Bowstrings of Spirit-Filled Preaching, Unforgettable Résumé, Preparing to Lead, Financing Vision, Beginning the Journey, Explore the Call,* and *Isolation in Ministry.* He enjoys reading and writing in the Colorado wilderness and spending time with his wife, Rhonda, and their adult children and grandchildren. You can reach Gene through www.generoncone.org.

May the LORD, the God who gives breath to all living things, appoint someone over this community to go out and come in before them, one who will lead them out and bring them in, so the LORD's people will not be like sheep without a shepherd.
Numbers 27:16-17 (NIV)

Table of Contents

1. Sons of Issachar 7

2. Why Leaders Neglect Succession Planning 13

3. Courageous Intentionality 21

4. Four Succession Models 37

5. The Growth of Mentored Success 43

6. The Stages of Mentored Succession 49

7. Church Governance & Minimal Requirements . 59

8. Family Members and Mentored Succession 67

9. Pros and Cons of Professional Search Firms 77

10. Standout Literature 85

11. Want to Learn More? 89

End Notes 91

1

Sons of Issachar

"All these men understood the signs of the times and knew the best course for Israel to take."
1 Chronicles 12:32 (NLT)

I never worried about Highpoint's future until my 23-year-old son Geno, and Highpoint's youth pastor, died from cancer in 2016. Neither I nor the board ever spoke formally about him as my successor. Yes, hypothetical comments were made on the wings of appreciation, but nothing formal. However, Geno grew up in the church and was respected and loved by all generations. I subconsciously assumed he would be there to help the church through the storm if something ever happened to me. I never imagined he would beat me to heaven.

Geno's early death made me more aware of my own mortality and the need to prepare Highpoint for something they did not have much experience in—finding a pastor. In over 86 years, Highpoint only had seven pastors. The last two of us led since 1975, which means that in 43 years, the church had only assembled a pastoral search committee once. Highpoint might be good at many things, but it did not have the opportunity to become skilled at pastoral transitions.

The Holy Spirit convicted me that I had invested more time preparing for a Sunday morning message than I had preparing the church to thrive without me. I found myself praying the same prayer Moses whispered in the mid-season of his own life.

"May the Lord, the God who gives breath to all living things, appoint someone over this community to go out and come in before them, one who will lead them out and bring them in, so the Lord's people will not be like sheep without a shepherd." (Numbers 27:16-17, NIV)

If you are reading this, you are probably a pastor sensing something is wrong or outdated with our current pastoral selection process. You know all leaders, including yourself, will one day move on. You are becoming anxious about tossing all your hard work and sacrifice on the gambling table of chance. You sense there must be a better way. Like the sons of Issachar during Israel's first leadership transition, you know it is time for a new approach to keep your church moving forward in health and growth. I know because I have been there. That is why I have spent many years studying transition models and coaching hundreds of churches through pastoral transitions that leave them stronger instead of weaker. I hope this book will help you consider a different model for your church to avoid the normal declines in morale, attendance, and giving associated with most leadership transitions. I also pray that when God initiates transition in your own life, your church will be stronger and healthier on the other side.

Even healthy churches in pastoral transition experience a 10-15 percent decline in attendance and a slightly lower decrease in tithes and offerings. In nearly all cases, it will take the new pastor one to two years to regain these losses. However, a few churches defy gravity and grow in morale, attendance, and income following a leadership transition. These churches have three things in common. First, they have a written transition plan. Second, they know who the successor is before the vacancy occurs. Third, the outgoing pastor is emotionally ready, supportive of the transition, and committed to its success. This third ingredient is the deal breaker. Without it, the church will experience decreased morale, attendance, and income despite possessing the first two.

Bestselling author and business consultant Peter Drucker once said, "The ingredient most missing in churches today is a plan of succession."[1] However, having a plan is only half the battle. It is also important to note that pastoral transition specialists William Vanderbloemen and Warren Bird confess that the existence of a transition plan is not a guarantee that it will succeed. Their experience brought them to conclude that "In the end, most of the success of a pastoral transition rises and falls on the shoulders of the outgoing pastor."[2] However, knowledge is power, and this resource can give you a strategic advantage and a greater likelihood for success in your church's transition journey.

The best place to start is to read this book and then ask the Holy Spirit to give you wisdom in vetting a plan with a small advance team from your leadership community. Because each situation is different, it would be impossible to produce a template that would fit your own context. However, this short book will help you get the wheels turning and give you a place to start.

In addition to leading my own mentored succession while pastoring, I have resourced hundreds of churches as a regional denominational leader. With the Lord's help and the Spirit's leading, history can also find you ready for what can be your finest hour.

MAKING IT REAL
Prayer, Reflection, and Action Items

1. How much time have you spent preparing your current ministry to thrive in your absence compared to other time investments you regularly make in pastoral ministry?
2. Is your church's organizational knowledge and experience concerning pastoral transitions sufficient to ensure success? If not, what can be done now to move the needle in this area?
3. Even healthy churches engaged in a pastoral transition experience a 10-15 percent decline in attendance and a slightly lower decrease in tithes and offerings. In nearly all cases, it will take the new pastor one to two years to regain these losses. How might these losses deprive your church of future opportunities?
4. How does the emotional readiness and support of the outgoing pastor affect the success of a pastoral transition?
5. Why is it important for a church to identify a successor before a vacancy occurs, and how can this practice benefit the church in the long run?
6. What role does the Holy Spirit play in preparing and executing a pastoral transition?
7. How can churches mitigate the typical morale, attendance, and income declines during a leadership transition? What strategies or practices might be helpful?
8. Peter Drucker and William Vanderbloemen emphasize the importance of having a succession

plan. How can church leaders ensure that their transition plans are both comprehensive and adaptable to their unique context?
9. In what ways can this chapter guide you in developing a successful transition strategy? How might you apply these insights to your own leadership situation?
10. What is your most significant "aha moment" or takeaway from this chapter?

2

Why Leaders Neglect Succession Planning

Some things are easier said than done, and succession planning is one of the hardest. Moses trained, empowered, and released Joshua. The Bible mentions the names of 19 of King David's sons, but David mentored Solomon to succeed him. Elijah mentored Elisha, Paul mentored Timothy, and Barnabas mentored John Mark. Even Jesus prepared His disciples to succeed Him. However, despite the biblical precedence for mentored succession, the process is difficult for most leaders to begin. Why might seasoned ministers neglect this noble task?

1. **Fearful procrastination.** Unfortunately, some ministers allow fear to suffocate their faith. They worry that succession planning means they are no longer relevant or that it will result in them leading in a lame-duck status. Some fear it will deprive them of the joys of ministry or the opportunity to depart on their own terms. Others

dread a future where they are not in control, leading the charge, financially stable, or lose the coveted title of "Lead Pastor." However, time never relieves us of the obligation to live by faith. Abraham understood this in his senior years and *"obeyed and went, even though he did not know where he was going"* (Hebrews 11:8 NIV). Waiting until you are sure all your questions are answered is not faith. The same God who cared for and directed you in the early days of your calling will continue to do so in your golden years.

2. **Unreasonable prerequisites.** Sometimes, ministers neglect succession planning because they wait for the perfect situation to materialize. Often, these triggers are as unreasonable as they are unlikely. They may wait for the perfect season, the perfect person, or the perfect opportunity. Other times, they hold out for assured financial stability, a convenient timeline, or a promised severance. A few wait so long for an ideal scenario that time melts like an ice cube in the desert. There is no better day than today to start prayerful planning. Scripture encourages us to *"not despise these small beginnings, for the Lord rejoices to see the work begin." (Zechariah 4:10, NLT)*

3. **Surrender of critical mass.** Critical mass is the lowest amount of resources required for an organization to grow and thrive independently. The saddest stories about planned succession are those of ministers who allow the church to

decline numerically, financially, and spiritually to the point where planned succession is either unattractive to a qualified successor or impossible for the church to accomplish. If they are not careful, these churches may echo the regret of God's people who said, *"The harvest is past, the summer has ended, and we are not saved." (Jeremiah 8:20, NIV)*

4. **Deferred opportunity.** Some effective leaders enjoy a long tenure of stable leadership that may last decades. However, if they are not intentional about planned succession, they can outlive their ability to be a change agent. The lack of strategic planning and mentoring can result in the next generation aging out while waiting on the bench. As a result, the church cannot benefit from those who could have kept it relevant, current, and multigenerational. Consequently, the church must now jump two generations in a single bound. "Carpe diem" is a Latin phrase that means "seize the day." In this case, however, some ministers defer opportunity until the day is lost.

5. **Absence of release.** Other ministers have a philosophical belief that succession planning should only be started after they feel a release from their current ministry. They are not against succession planning but do not see a need because they still possess a strong call, vision, energy level, and mandate to lead the church.

They postpone the inevitable, believing it must be obvious before action is taken.

6. **Misplaced identity.** A few ministers have allowed their current title or ministry to become the centerpiece of their identity. Their status, belonging, and self-esteem are derived from their work rather than their relationship with God and family. To them, succession planning means the loss of self-worth, fulfillment, and happiness. Because they cannot imagine being or doing anything other than their current role, they hold on with white knuckles until misfortune pries them loose.

7. **Emotional anchors.** All of us journey through life with emotional baggage—even ministers. Whether it is fear, insecurity, disappointment, deferred hope, or sadness, some ministers allow their emotional anchors to keep them and their church close to the harbor. In Numbers 27:15-17 Moses prayed that God would send a successor to lead the nation, but when God took him up on the offer, Moses struggled with letting go, complained, and lashed out at others (Deuteronomy 3:23-27). In the end, however, Moses prevailed over his dark side and obeyed God (Numbers 27:27). You can also.

8. **Disobedient existence.** God commanded Moses to prepare for a leadership transition by mentoring Joshua to be his successor. Numbers

27:12-23 and Deuteronomy 3:23-28 record this command punctuated with the phrase, *"Moses did as the Lord commanded him."* Many leaders know God has told them to start preparing a successor. They know it in their heart, may even long to be released from the heavy burden, and feel the tide turning in their ministries, but they cannot bring themselves to obey. As a result, they choose to embrace convenient disobedience rather than joyful adventure.

Good and wise succession planning need not limit a leader's options or stamp an expiration date on their forehead. Moses continued to lead the people of Israel and prepare his successor for several decades after God told him to equip Joshua. The important thing was that he started, and once he did, momentum carried him along and the Spirit filled in the blanks.

MAKING IT REAL
Prayer, Reflection, and Action Items

1. What are some common fears or anxieties you have concerning succession planning?
2. What steps can you take to confront and move beyond these fears?
3. What are some examples of unreasonable prerequisites that might delay succession planning? What unreasonable prerequisites do you find yourself embracing?
4. How can neglecting succession planning contribute to a decline in your church's health and vitality, and what proactive measures can you take to avoid this scenario?
5. Why must leaders engage in succession planning even if they still feel energized and called to their current role? How can this approach benefit both you and your church?
6. In what ways might your own identity be tied to your current role, and how can understanding this help in addressing resistance to succession planning?
7. How can emotional baggage and personal struggles affect a leader's approach to succession planning? What strategies can be used to manage these emotional anchors effectively?
8. What does the example of Moses' response to God's command about succession teach us about obedience in leadership transitions, and how can you apply this lesson in your own context?

9. How can you confidentially start the succession planning process even when you need more clarification on all the details or answers?
10. What practical steps can you take to ensure that succession planning does not result in adverse outcomes such as decreased morale, giving, or attendance? How can these steps be integrated into the church's overall strategy?

3

Courageous Intentionality

Fear is the primary reason pastors fail to involve their boards in transition and succession planning. In their book, *The Elephant in the Boardroom: Speaking the Unspoken About Pastoral Transitions*, authors Weese and Crabtree spread blame a bit further saying, "Leaders on both sides of the board table must face the unhealthy part of themselves that threatens a successful pastoral transition . . . Although we would like to assume that a strong commitment obviates a shadow side to the Christian leader, all the evidence shows it does not."[3] However, there are often justifiable reasons for these unsettling emotions. Every situation is different and will require a leader to courageously strike a balance between Spirit and flesh as well as faith and fear. I will share how I navigated my way through this minefield in hopes that it will help you find God's will in your own context.

Why Risk Is Justified

These discussions have legitimate risks, and not all board members are spiritually or emotionally mature enough to handle them. These risks include:

Impatience. Instead of a succession plan being considered a strategic plan for the future, its existence has the potential of becoming an "outstanding task" in need of premature execution dates, progress, and constant attention.

Disunity. Those who have their own agenda can use succession planning to expedite their pastor's departure. In this case, the plan becomes a "coup" in disguise. Every church has a few spiritually immature leaders who choose to be activists, critics, and pursuers of greater influence. Succession planning can become a playground for the immature and divisive.

Instability. Rumors of attention being given to a succession plan can create a culture of apprehension and uncertainty in the church. A perceived sense of instability can cause valuable staff members to secretly explore employment possibilities elsewhere. Large givers can feel unsure and restrain their generosity. Volunteers can be cautious about making commitments, and fringe attenders and members who feel connected to the lead pastor may start shopping for a new church home.

Fear and insecurity. Statistics show that nothing influences the success of a pastoral transition or succession plan more than the support and enthusiasm of the outgoing pastor. Author Gary Smith is convinced that "most of the success of a pastoral transition rises and falls on the shoulders of the outgoing pastor."[4] Succession expert Jerry David claims many transitions are unintentionally sabotaged by insecure leaders who undermine their successors in a way that contributes to their failure.[5] If a transition depends upon the outgoing pastor's support, the pastor and their spouse must be emotionally, financially, intellectually, and spiritually ready. Some may be more ready to be relieved of their responsibilities than they are of their influence.

Why Courageous Intentionality Is Needed

It sits on my desk and reminds me that I am part of something bigger than myself. It is a log slice from a tree that gave my family shelter in the national forest. After 109 years, the mighty tree finally fell. A friend was kind enough to make the journey, cut a timber slice, and use a high-powered magnifying glass to count its rings. Knowing it was my son Geno's favorite camping spot, he and his wife gave it to me as a gift. This pillar of the forest lived from 1909 until 2018. Much like my son's premature death, it reminds me that everything in this world is temporary—even pastors.

Outside of its sentimental value, the tree slice speaks to me about my role and contribution as a pastor. The tree is like a church and its rings are like seasons of its lifespan. Seasons of growth produced rings with larger spaces between them. This resulted from the tree being blessed with favorable temperatures and rain. Seasons of dormancy created rings that are tight and close together. The tree suffered through drought, long winters, or limited sunlight during these seasons. Rings scarred by burn marks reflect fires the tree endured, and dark discoloring reveals a temporary infestation of insects or fungus. The older the tree, the slower it grows because its roots have grown deep enough to have to compete with other trees for nutrients, resources, and water. Though older, the tree is more stable and may provide shelter for over a hundred years, like this one.

However, the most profound story the rings tell is one of perseverance. The rings remind us that our role as leaders in life is temporary. Some pastors ignore 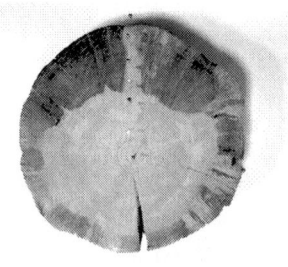 preceding rings and mistakenly think the tree's history began the day they arrived. Others believe the tree's sole purpose is to build their personal legacy or feed their voracious egos. Unfortunately, some leave the tree in distress while others leave wide and healthy rings. Most leave rings of modest but consistent growth. Ultimately, the fires, floods, or growing seasons are not as important as the question, "Will our contribution cause the tree to outlive us?"

I pastored Highpoint for nearly 17 years. At the time of my departure, the church was 86 years old and only had seven pastors. The last three pastors made up 62 years of the church's history. That is why I framed the tree slice and hung it on the wall in my office. The tree reminds me that pastoral ministry is not about me but the church's survival. It reminds me that although we will face storms, droughts, and fires, the tree must survive! It reminds me that there were rings before me and rings that will follow me. But my stewardship of the tree, not the width of my rings, tells the truest story. Therefore, I concluded that for Highpoint, the need outweighed the risks regarding succession planning.

Justified Fear and Courageous Intentionality

Even though I was only 50 years of age with no intention of leaving or retiring soon, I decided to start leading differently. The thought occurred to me that every pastor is an interim pastor, no matter how long their tenure. I started leading as if I were a long-term interim pastor. Our governance did not give me the right to select my successor. However, I could lead in a way that would stage an eventual transition for success. I could prepare and resource those charged with finding the next pastor. I could mentor in a way that presented the possibility of both internal and external candidates.

Churches can be like garages in that they accumulate lots of "stuff" and unfinished projects. Mine was the same. Without others knowing it, I decided to make a list of problems I knew a future successor would have to tackle. Then, I took every one of them on in a patient and methodical manner. After being at Highpoint for nearly 17 years and leading the church through the construction of a new campus across town, I felt I had earned enough trust to absorb any fallout fighting these battles might bring. The list consisted of things such as:

1. **Governance.** Addressing governance issues and rewriting the church bylaws. This took me two years.
2. **Policy.** Updating financial policies, board etiquette, and operating procedures.
3. **Neutralization.** Diplomatically neutralizing the influence of problem, divisive, or high-maintenance leaders.
4. **Accountability.** Confronting and realigning committees or ministries that had drifted from their mission and/or accountability structure.
5. **Board.** Training my board about how difficult pastoral ministry really is and helping them become more supportive and helpful to spiritual leadership in the future.
6. **Planned abandonment.** Giving a few ministries I started a decent burial. God had given me the

vision and energy to lead them, but I felt sustaining them would become a burden to someone who did not share my sense of divine mandate.

7. **Exit strategies.** Formulating exit strategies for large financial pledges and stale partnerships that no longer brought life and energy to our missions and outreach ministries.
8. **Empowerment.** Expressing financial faith to engage highly gifted and diverse staff pastors and then ushering them into the "inner circle" of our leadership structure.
9. **Tribal storytelling.** Mentoring promising staff and volunteers to become organizational DNA carriers for Highpoint's future.
10. **Strategic planning.** Writing a 140-page manual on how the church would find a new pastor if something unexpected happened to me.

All these things created new margin and opportunities for whoever would follow me. However, the most surprising result from this process was that Highpoint started experiencing another wave of numerical and financial growth. Please do not misunderstand; there is never one reason a church is growing. If a church is growing, it is always the result of several factors. However, the checking account and attendance records seemed to confirm that God was honoring this courageous outlook.

Building an Advance Team

Despite being met with the Lord's favor, there was one mountain to climb. I enjoyed working with a large board of 12 people (including myself). Although I desperately wanted to work arm in arm with my entire board to develop and train them for an eventual transition, I could not get a release from the Lord to do so. I felt some of our leaders may lack the spiritual sensitivity to deal with this issue in a way that would honor the Lord. Two had already exhibited an inability to keep confidence regarding board decisions. Their desire to be liked often blinded them from Kingdom opportunities. I felt their lack of self-control predicted what I could expect in addressing the higher levels of confidentiality required in mentored succession. Paul seems to confirm my caution when he told the Corinthians, *"There must be factions among you in order that those who are genuine among you may be recognized." (1 Corinthians 11:19, ESV)*

I asked the Lord in prayer for two years to either grow or remove them so I could have peace about revealing the 140-page transition manual to the entire board. Until He did, I engaged a small team of board officers and one alternate who already had my unequivocal trust. I asked them to pray about signing a strict confidentiality agreement and serve as an advance team to train and coach the board if anything ever happened to me. We met several times in my home to work through the manual, pray, and discuss applications. I will forever cherish the memories, tears, prayers, laughter, and wisdom that converged in those meetings! When God called me to serve as district superintendent, Highpoint already had an advance team of mature board members to start the process and keep things on track.

Following are a few talking points from the memo I gave the advance team after opening our first meeting in prayer.

SIGNIFICANT CONCERNS. *Allow me to begin our meeting by bringing up a few concerns I have regarding this risky process of introducing you to a succession plan if anything ever happens to me.*

1. ***Confidentiality.*** *Having a good succession plan does not guarantee its success. I have not shared this with the entire board because I am concerned about a few who may lack self-control and the ability to maintain confidentiality. Our church is growing, and I do not want to risk losing momentum because a few people have loose lips.*
2. ***Respect.*** *I do not want to be penalized for being proactive and putting these things in writing. Some consultants advise against sharing a succession plan with the board before it is needed. Even churches that have plans only have a 50 percent success rate for the following reasons:*
    - ***Impatience.*** *Instead of the plan serving as a contingency, it is considered an unresolved task in need of execution dates, progress, and constant attention.*

- ***Disunity.*** *Those who oppose the pastor or have a different agenda can use the plan as a way to expedite his/her departure.*
- ***Instability.*** *Rumors of attention being given to a succession plan can create a culture of apprehension, fear, and uncertainty in the church. The perceived sense of uncertainty can cause exceptional staff members to update their résumés and shop for employment elsewhere. Givers can feel unsure and start withholding offerings, restraining their generosity, or insulating themselves from visionary appeals. Volunteers can be cautious about making commitments, and people who feel connected to the lead pastor may start looking for a new church home.*
- ***Fear.*** *Statistics show that nothing influences the success of a succession plan more than the outgoing pastor's support and enthusiasm. If a transition depends on the outgoing pastor's support, the pastor must be emotionally, financially, intellectually, and spiritually ready.*

I can trust our board officers. We have served together for nearly two decades. You love me, and I love you. Unless I disqualify myself or am ineffective, I want to decide when I leave and not be pressured to establish a timeline. I am confident we can overcome all four of these potential threats.

3. **Transition fund.** *The fact is that EVERY pastor, whether they realize it or not, is an interim pastor. Because transition is inevitable, expenses related to it are also unavoidable. When it comes to financing a transition, there is always a "best case," "likely case," and "worst case"*

scenario. For various reasons we will discuss later, I believe Highpoint will need to plan for a healthy transition fund. Over a year ago, I used an existing but empty church bank account to start a pastoral transition fund. I envision this fund being used to help underwrite transition expenses and finance a new pastor's early initiatives. Rhonda and I have already made the first significant donation to this fund, and we are asking you to consider taking eight weeks to match ours and do the same. In the Old Testament, the waters of the Jordan did not part until the leaders walked in first (Joshua 3:13). Would you talk with your spouse about matching our gift in the next eight weeks?

4. **Inexperience.** *Pastoral departures are usually unpredictable. By the time a board learns the pastor is leaving, there is little time to educate oneself, develop systems, and learn from experts. In over 86 years, Highpoint has been pastored by only seven men. The last two of Highpoint's pastors have led since 1975, which means that in the previous 43 years, the church has only assembled a pastoral search committee once!* ***Highpoint may be good at many things, but we do not have enough experience to be skilled at pastoral transitions.*** *That is why I have spent many months reading, researching, and writing a board-led succession plan that gives the church options and direction. I have educated myself on the most significant obstacles and best practices of pastoral transitions. I have interviewed wise leaders, district officials, and peers regarding board-led succession plans. I have also considered how Highpoint's unique needs, culture, and history will shape our needs in a successful transition. That is why I wrote a 13-stage plan to serve the board as a guide but not necessarily as a rule.*

I want to coach our board officers and one alternate on the contents of this manual so they can serve as guides to the board if it should ever be needed.

COACHING PLAN. *I want to take this group on the following journey to provide an advance team that can usher the board and church through a pastoral transition when it occurs. This would involve the following:*

1. ***A Commitment of Confidentiality.*** *Have all four of us sign a mutual and binding nondisclosure agreement.*
2. **Meeting #1: Clarification.** *Discuss these concerns, agree on how to proceed, and introduce six chapters in what I will call a "partial reveal." I know this will be a lot for you to take in all at once, so I want to unveil it in small amounts, starting with six critical chapters.*
3. **Partial reveal.** *I will introduce the six critical chapters of the manual and allow you to read them independently before our next meeting.*
4. **Meeting #2.** *Discussion of the first six chapters of the partial reveal.*
5. **Full reveal.** *Introduce the entire 140-page manual and allow you to read it independently.*
6. **Meeting #3.** *Discuss the first half of the manual consisting of Chapters 1-19.*
7. **Meeting #4.** *Discuss Appendixes A-Z.*
8. **Full release.** *Distribute the full electronic version to the officers and alternate with the understanding that we are all under the obligation of the nondisclosure*

agreement until I decide to give the full board access, die, leave, or become unable to pastor.

Each meeting ended up being about three hours in length. I have never regretted doing this and found that each advance team member elevated their level, distinction, and service. They became more sensitive, wise, supportive, and willing to lead their peers in discerning between better and best.

Years later, Highpoint's new pastor has led the church to higher attendance, giving, and engagement levels. Under the leadership of my successor, they have also added a third Sunday morning worship service. I feel so thankful to the Lord each time I visit that I can hardly hold back the tears. Ecclesiastes 3 teaches us that all things have a time and season. It was the Spirit's timing. You will need to discern your own time for courageous intentionality. When you do, this resource can serve as a springboard to develop your own plan with your own leadership community or advance team.

MAKING IT REAL
Prayer, Reflection, and Action Items

1. What fears might prevent pastors from involving their boards in succession planning, and how can they be addressed or mitigated in your context?
2. What potential risks are associated with succession planning, such as impatience or disunity, and how can these be managed effectively?
3. How can you emotionally, financially, and spiritually prepare yourself to lead a successful succession plan?
4. How does the tree metaphor with its rings illustrate the concept of pastoral leadership and succession, and what can be learned about leaving a lasting impact from this metaphor?
5. Why might it be necessary for a pastor to view their role as temporary, and how can this perspective influence your approach to succession planning?
6. What are some actionable steps you can take to start planning for succession even if you do not intend to leave your position soon?
7. How might your church's governance model impact the steps of a successful succession plan, and what are some key areas to address proactively?
8. What role does confidentiality play in succession planning, and how might you

ensure sensitive information is handled appropriately?
9. In what ways can an advanced team or small group of trusted leaders assist in preparing for a pastoral transition, and how can their effectiveness be ensured?
10. What are the benefits of creating a transition fund, and how can it support a smooth pastoral changeover in your context?

4

Four Succession Models

Many transition specialists, denominational leaders, and local churches are starting to question whether the traditional method of pastoral selection is effective. The model of bringing in outsiders with no understanding of the church culture, community, and congregation seems to be creating a continuing cycle of short-term pastorates. Andrew Flowers' research and book entitled, *Leading Through Succession: Why Pastoral Leadership Is Key to a Healthy Transition on Pastoral Transition* sounds the alarm:

> *"Something seems to be horribly wrong with the process of appointing pastors. It's the epidemic no one wants to talk about and it's not uncommon for churches to go through two or three sacrificial lambs before someone is able to stick."* [6]

Transition experts Carolyn Weese and Russell Crabtree complain:

> *"The current model of pastoral transition, left over from a time when organizational learning was not as important, does not help congregations protect what is healthy and retain what they have learned. It is the organizational equivalent of burning down the community library every time a new mayor is elected."* [7]

Mark Moore of Christ's Church of the Valley in Peoria, Arizona cries out:

> *"There is a black hole in church leadership transition strategy. What we don't know how to do is transition from first generational leaders to second generational successors. It's not that we have no theory; it's that we have few models to follow in churches where the stakes are the highest because of the church's influence and visibility."* [8]

This frustration has resulted in the growing popularity of other succession models. Author Terry Roberts says:

> *"There is no one-size-fits-all model. Plans differ just as the churches they serve differ. However, the best plans have one thing in common: They combine the wisdom and stability of a seasoned leader and the vision and energy of a young leader. As such, they help the church not only go through the challenge of change but also grow through it."* [9]

A 2019 Barna research project found that *"while the majority of church transitions occur because a pastor initiates their departure, planning ahead for an inevitable transition makes a big difference in congregants' experiences."* [10]

Most churches' bylaws embrace a traditional search committee-driven plan. However, several other models of strategic succession are gaining popularity and proving effective. They are listed briefly for information.

1. **Board-driven succession.** The board or committee, acting as the search team, interviews prospective candidates and recommends one of them to the congregation to be voted upon by the membership.

2. **Relayed succession.** When the pastor resigns, the board selects an interim pastor to serve for one to two years while an extended search process is undertaken. The interim pastor is not considered as a candidate but tasked with preparing the church for the future pastor. In this model, the interim pastor could best be described as a relay runner in the short leg of a long race. This model tends to be more prevalent in liturgical churches.

3. **Mentored succession.** The lead pastor and the board collaborate to select a person (current staff or future staff member) who is mentored and trained to one day lead the church. There is a focus on identifying a divinely called "DNA carrier" who understands the church, has proven themselves effective, is mentored by the outgoing pastor, and is loved and trusted by the people.

This model is becoming increasingly popular in churches with over 500 attendees.

4. **Scheduled succession.** The lead pastor informs the board one to two years before they intend to step down or retire. The first year is spent searching for a successor, and the second year is spent mentoring that person to lead. This plan works best when the lead pastor is near retirement age and has a specific start and end date that is agreed upon by all (pastor, successor, and board).

MAKING IT REAL
Prayer, Reflection, and Action Items

1. What are the primary limitations of the traditional method of pastoral selection, and how do these limitations impact a church's health, stability, and effectiveness?
2. How does Andrew Flowers' observation about the frequency of short-term pastorates reflect broader issues in pastoral transitions? What might be contributing to this trend?
3. In what ways does the traditional pastoral transition model fail to preserve a church's organizational knowledge and health, according to Carolyn Weese and Russell Crabtree?
4. What are the advantages and potential drawbacks of a board-driven succession model? How can churches ensure that this model is implemented effectively?
5. In a relayed succession model, what role does the interim pastor play, and how can their contribution be maximized during the transition?
6. What are the three critical characteristics of a successful mentored succession model, and what contribution do you think each one plays in the success quotient?
7. How does a scheduled succession model address the timing and planning of a pastoral transition? What factors should be considered to ensure its success?
8. How might the lack of a one-size-fits-all succession model impact the planning and

execution of pastoral transitions in different churches?
9. How can you and your board assess whether a mentored succession plan or another model best fits your church's specific needs and context?
10. How can the wisdom of experienced leaders and the fresh perspective of younger leaders be integrated to support a smooth transition and growth in the church?

5

The Growth of Mentored Succession

Mentored succession is the most promising wave of the future when it comes to pastoral transition. Why? First, because it is more collaborative than the traditional model. The existing pastor and the board work together to find a potential successor. Secondly, because the successor is a DNA carrier. By that, I mean they not only know the church's culture but have served on staff before their election and earned the respect of the congregation. Thirdly, unlike the traditional model of bringing in an outsider while the church grinds its gears for two to three years, mentored succession can make the church stronger instead of weaker. It helps the church gain momentum instead of suffering the normal decreases in morale, giving, and attendance.

In mentored succession, the lead pastor and board collaborate and select a person (current staff or future staff member) to be mentored and trained to one day lead the church. This model has proven successful and is gaining popularity in larger churches where the outgoing pastor has had an effective and long-term ministry for over ten years. Several books are authored by transition specialists and pastors who have successfully navigated the uncertain waters of mentored succession. Author Terry Roberts has documented that the model has been a norm in many large churches in Asian cultures.[11] Glen Wolf is one of the first millennials to have made an academic and thoughtful contribution to this body of work. In his doctoral thesis, he gives the following four reasons why succession planning must become a priority.[12]

- Succession is inevitable in every church.
- Succession is generationally urgent.
- Succession is most important in ministry.
- Succession is a topic most pastors are unprepared and uninformed about.

Although the entire process takes longer than a traditional search, when done right, it has proven to insulate the church from declines in attendance, volunteerism, engagement, and giving. Many churches using the mentored succession model have grown on the other side of the transition. I often refer to this benefit as defying gravity.

However, defying gravity requires the church to do the following three things.
- It must know who the successor is before the existing pastor resigns.

- It must have a written plan with details, processes, steps, and mutually confirmed agreements.
- The outgoing pastor must be privately and publicly supportive of the successor. The outgoing pastor must also accept that the plan's goal is to successfully transition a new leader into the future and not a way to extend their own tenure or legacy.

All three ingredients are essential, but the last one is the deal breaker. Even if a church has the first two elements, the plan will fail without the third.

MAKING IT REAL
Prayer, Reflection, and Action Items

1. How does the collaborative nature of mentored succession compare to the traditional pastoral transition model? What are the key benefits of this approach?
2. In what ways does being a "DNA carrier" enhance a potential successor's effectiveness in leading a church compared to an outsider?
3. What specific factors contribute to the momentum gained during a mentored succession, and how does it counteract the typical declines experienced during transitions?
4. How might your church identify and prepare a suitable successor for a mentored succession model?
5. Why might mentored succession be particularly effective in larger churches with long-term pastors? What unique challenges do these churches face that this model addresses?
6. What three elements make up a successful mentored succession plan, and how can these elements be effectively implemented in your setting?
7. How does having a written plan with detailed processes and steps contribute to the success of a mentored succession model?
8. Why is the outgoing pastor's support crucial to the success of a mentored succession plan? How can this support be effectively demonstrated both privately and publicly?

9. What are the potential consequences if the outgoing pastor prioritizes extending their own tenure or legacy over the successful transition of a new leader?
10. How can churches ensure that they are prepared for succession planning if they are currently unprepared or uninformed about the process?

Stages of Mentored Succession

Although each mentored succession story is different, I have noticed a few common denominators and intentional processes employed in successful handoffs. I have compiled and summarized these best practices in the following seven stages.

Stage 1: Embracing change. This stage involves the current pastor becoming ready, willing, and able to let go. This is the most critical step because it requires the leader to be able to let go of responsibility and influence. Some can let go of one of those, but a smooth transition requires a person to be able to release both gracefully. Honest self-reflection, repeated years of plateauing or declining ministry, waning vision, a prolonged period of being in maintenance mode, and decreasing energy and physical ability all play a part in coming to grips with this reality.

One leader told me his moment of enlightenment came when he realized he had not killed or birthed a new ministry in over five years. At the end of the day, all leaders must be open to hearing God's voice and moving forward with the same faith and surrender they possessed in their early days of ministry. God instructed Abraham when he was 75 years old to "*go from your people and your father's household to the land I will show you*" (Genesis 12:1). Even in the twilight years of Abraham's life, God required him to walk off the map and enter an unknown season without promises or certainty. Age never relieves us of our obligation to live and transition our ministries by faith.

Stage 2: Finding Joshua. Stage two involves the lead pastor and board collaborating to identify a person (current staff or future staff member) who is mentored and trained to one day lead the church. There are several ways leaders have achieved this, but God's Word gives us an excellent model. After Moses was told that he would not be leading the children of Israel into the Promised Land, he prayed that God would appoint a new leader for the nation (Numbers 27:16-17). The Lord instructed Moses to mentor Joshua to succeed him in leadership.

> "*Take Joshua son of Nun, a man in whom is <u>the spirit of leadership</u> and lay your hand on him.*" *(Numbers 27:18, NIV, emphasis added)*

What is the "spirit of leadership"? Scholars are unsure, but the context suggests five characteristics successors should have.

- **History of faithfulness.** Joshua had already proven himself faithful to God, Moses, and the nation's mission. He had served faithfully as Moses's right-hand man since Mount Sinai (Exodus 33:11). He was not influenced by negative peer pressure and was willing to be among the courageous minority (Numbers 14:5-9). He won battles, raised up military commanders, and constantly grew into his calling. He had already proven himself faithful in leadership positions, was loyal to Moses, and was attuned to where God was leading the nation. The selection of a successor must be based on more than potential. They must have a track record of success.

- **Successful followership.** As strange as it may sound, the best leaders have been successful followers in prior seasons of their development. The capacity to follow reveals that a leader can be loyal to something other than themselves, their own ideas, or personal passions. It also shows they know how to live on the implementation side of the leadership equation. Anyone can dream dreams that others must implement, but successful followers see how the parts are connected in order to get things done. Not all followers are leaders, but all outstanding leaders have a history of faithfully following in different contexts.

- **DNA carrier.** To lead into the future, the successor must know, value, and appreciate the church's culture. Being a "DNA" carrier does not mean they will not make changes. It does mean change is made with a keen sensitivity to where the church has been while also knowing where it needs to be.
- **Proven results.** Joshua had more than God's favor; he also had Moses's confidence and the trust of clan leaders from each of Israel's tribes. Why? Because he won battles, brought wins to the table, and had a track record of success (Joshua 11:16-23). If something was entrusted to Joshua, it became effective, grew, and contributed to the nation's success. Unfortunately, we live in a day when optics are valued more than results. Leaders are often judged more by their trendy vocabulary and slick appearance than their track record. There is a difference between faithfulness and results. A leader without results is nothing more than an untested theoretician. Theoreticians usually have ideas, vocabulary, and speech that are more impressive than the results column on their résumé. However, Joshua could deliver wins, raise up leaders, and inspire others to follow. That is why the people trusted and followed him into the nation's future.
- **Divine giftings.** The Lord said Joshua had "*the spirit of leadership.*" Scholars are uncertain as to what that may mean. There appears to be two options. The original Hebrew word used for

"spirit" could be applied to mean either "courage to lead" or a "God-given gift of leadership." Either way, it appears God anointed Joshua in a way that empowered him with courage and leadership. I personally think it implies the overlapping of natural talent and supernatural anointing. Joshua was blessed to have both.

When it comes to finding the right Joshua, Bryant Wright compares the process to knowing when someone has found the right person to marry. "You just know," says Wright.[13]

Stage 3: Wading into culture. This stage involves a testing time where the potential successor is given a portfolio, placed on the teaching team, and then works on staff to determine if they are compatible with the church, mentoring pastor, board, staff, and the local community. It also is a time to evaluate their ability to learn culture, ask good questions, and earn the confidence of key leaders. At the end of this time, the lead pastor and board decide if the potential successor can advance to the next stage or if they need to keep looking.

Stage 4: Testing compatibility. This step involves the potential candidate continuing in a determined portfolio while being exposed to every significant facet of the church's administration, financial structure, ministries, neighborhood, and community at large to develop cultural and organizational mastery. This critical step aims to determine cultural, philosophical, theological, and stylistic compatibility.

The prophet Amos warns about ignoring this season: *"Can two people walk together without agreeing on the direction?"* (Amos 3:3 NLT). Glen Wolf summarizes this process as a hands-on, four-stage progression of mentoring. First, the mentor does it, and the mentee watches; second, the mentee helps the mentor do it; third, the mentor helps the mentee do it; and fourth, the mentee does it, and the mentor watches.[14]

Stage 5: Organizational confirmation involves the potential candidate being interviewed and considered by the board as "pastor-elect." To gain organizational confirmation, some may even present this plan to the voting members and ask them to endorse the board's sentiment through a vote. If selected, the pastor-elect continues to serve as the lead pastor's second in command and right arm until a predetermined date or the lead pastor resigns, retires, or dies. In this stage, the board fulfills its duty to find a new pastoral candidate *early* instead of waiting until *after* a pastor departs as traditionally done.

Stage 6: Facilitating success. This stage is a scheduled season where the lead pastor employs their authority, credibility, and trust to implement changes the successor will need to be successful. This may include alterations in staff, structure, and finances that play to the successor's strengths and backfill their limitations. It also may involve giving ineffective, outdated, or leader-dependent ministries a graceful funeral. This allows the board and pastor to provide the pastor-elect with the highest likelihood of future success. Walter Harvey's book compares this stage of mentored succession to an alley-oop pass in basketball. Harvey claims mentored succession requires the predecessor to set up plays that selflessly allow their successor to slam dunk the ball and energize the team and the crowd simultaneously.[15]

Stage 7: The handoff. The last stage occurs when the lead pastor resigns, retires, or dies. At that time, the pastor-elect is immediately presented to the church as a candidate to be voted upon. The previous pastor's role is to transition into a new phase of ministry while lending influence to their successor. Jeff Adams pastored Graceway Church in Kansas City, Missouri, for 33 years. After a successful handoff to his successor, Jeff said, *"My success is inseparable from that of my successor... I was to use my influence to be the bridge for him to the congregation. I was to withdraw all of the funds from my credibility bank and use them to pave his road to success."*[16]

Most succession specialists agree that every church is different, and although steps are helpful, each plan must be customized to fit the needs and realities of their unique situation. In their book on the succession process, Vandebloemen and Bird warn, *"While succession is uniformly important and urgent, there is no uniform approach that works for all churches."* [17] The seven stages above are only a suggested springboard to help you determine your own plan with practical action steps.

MAKING IT REAL
Prayer, Reflection, and Action Items

1. What are the key indicators that a current pastor is ready to let go of responsibility and influence? What would be the hardest three things for you to release at this time in your journey?
2. How does the example of Abraham's call to move to an unknown land in his senior years illustrate the faith and surrender required for a successful pastoral transition? What kind of faith and surrender would be required of you in mentored succession?
3. This chapter identified five criteria a potential successor, or "Joshua," would need to possess. How might that criteria be tested in your ministry setting?
4. How important is it for a potential successor to be a "DNA carrier," and what five cultural DNA strands in your church would your future successor need to succeed?
5. This chapter presented the following seven potential stages of mentored succession.
    - Embracing change
    - Finding Joshua
    - Wading into culture
    - Testing compatibility
    - Organizational confirmation
    - Facilitating success
    - The handoff

What would be the goals and challenges of each stage in your ministry context?

6. Meditate upon younger leaders in your circle of relationships and write down the names of those with the highest potential to be your Joshua. Now, begin to pray that God would orchestrate a divine intersection with them or others who can be mentored to one day lead your church.

7. What are the critical components of organizational confirmation, and how might you and your church board effectively engage the congregation in this process?

8. In what ways could you facilitate success for your successor during the transition period? What specific changes might need to be implemented?

9. How does the analogy of the alley-oop pass in basketball relate to the process of facilitating success for a successor? How can the lead pastor ensure they set up their successor for success?

10. What are the essential elements of a successful handoff, and how can the outgoing pastor effectively use their influence to support their successor during this final stage?

Church Governance and Minimal Requirements

The availability of mentored succession will largely depend upon the church's governance structure, bylaws, and a few core competencies of everyone involved.

Church Governance

Governance is how a church makes decisions, who makes them, and the parameters of accountability. At first glance, it may seem that mentored succession favors independent churches and poses problems for churches with congregational forms of governance, where the bylaws require members to elect the lead pastor. However, contemporary examples can be found where different styles of church governance are able to embrace the mentored succession model through increased collaboration.

- **Presbyterian** governance delegates authority and responsibility to elected representatives authorized to act on behalf of the congregation. This form of governance requires the least amount of organizational-wide collaboration since the governing body is usually given great authority and empowered to act on behalf of church members.

- **Episcopal** governance is a hierarchical structure with one priest or bishop who answers to another who answers to another until there is one potentate at the top who has final authority. This form of governance can embrace mentored succession by planning ahead and seeking the blessing and cooperation of the bishop or organizational overseer.
- **Congregational** governance is the opposite of Episcopal. Church members meet to make all the decisions about budgets, ministries, policy, and even personnel. While everyone has a voice, these churches can be inundated with division and are often slow to change. This form of governance requires the most collaboration and methodical steps. Voting members must be persuaded that mentored succession is in the best interest of the church and given the opportunity to pre-approve the concept and steps of the process.
- **Hybrid Presbyterian/Congregational.** Most Evangelical churches embrace a hybrid Presbyterian/congregational form of church government. This hybrid model recognizes the membership as the final decision-making

body of the church but delegates authority and duties to others (lead pastor, board, and denominational affiliation) to act on their behalf. Power is delegated and, at times, even shared in overlapping areas. This enables the church to have sufficient accountability structures while, at the same time, benefit from a board of directors and being led by visionary leadership. It helps with being accountable, decisive, and responsive all at the same time. While this form requires collaboration, the membership can approve the process and provide additional confirmation if needed.

Pastor Dick Iverson of City Bible Church in Portland, Oregon, chose to use his church's governance to provide what he called "a three-fold witness."[18] After much prayer and deliberation, Iverson believed Frank Damazio was to be his successor. City Bible Church is an independent Charismatic church with a pastor-led governance (presbyterial model), thus not requiring the vote of the church members. However, Iverson saw the wisdom in taking the matter to the congregation for approval or affirmation. The three-fold witness ended up being experienced in the heart of the outgoing pastor (first confirmation), the conviction of the official board (second confirmation), and confirmed a third time through a vote of the church members.

Jeff Harlow pastored Crossroads Community Church in Kokomo, Indiana, for 35 years before investing three years mentoring an exterior candidate and outsider, Chris Duncan, into a strategic succession. Harlow embraced their hybrid presbyterian/congregational form of governance as a way to provide a "safety net" and designed three congregational votes at different stages of the succession process. Harlow gave the rationale for this procedure in his book:

> *"At some point in my leadership career, I decided to make voting my friend. I used votes to gain ownership and measure buy-in, not just to grab permission. If you don't have the people's approval of the new leader, you're fighting a battle you will not win. A power play at this point will put the very team and stakeholders you love and appreciate at risk as well as jeopardizing the very mission you're working to extend beyond your tenure."*[19]

Harlow already knew what the Barna Group would confirm in their 2019 research project entitled, *Leadership Transitions: How Churches Navigate Pastoral Change and Stay Healthy*, where they reported, "As a general rule, the higher the degree of congregants involvement, the more positive they feel about the final outcome."[20]

Minimal Competencies

Although mentored succession is new and proving to be very successful, it does require the following ingredients, which not all situations can provide.

1. **The total commitment of the outgoing pastor.** Gary Smith's book outlines the following five things the departing pastor must bring to the table if mentored succession is to work.[21]
   - **God's will.** The outgoing pastor must be convinced that the transition is God's will for *everyone* involved and be willing to devote the time and effort needed to ensure its success.
   - **Financial security.** The outgoing pastor must have a financial plan to provide for their family without reliance upon the church.
   - **Marital unity.** The outgoing pastor's spouse (and family) must fully support and help the successor succeed.
   - **Future ministry.** The outgoing pastor must have clear direction on the next stage of ministry. In other words, they must have identified the next chapter of their ministry.
   - **Humility.** The outgoing pastor must be prepared to meet the challenge with humility and see the church's success as more important than their own. Without humility on both sides of the equation, there will be no successful succession.

2. **Board involvement.** The collaboration and participation of the governing board in the plan and selection of the successor.
3. **A culture of honor.** Patience and respect for the outgoing pastor and the teachability of the successor. Both must be committed to building and maintaining a culture of honor that goes both ways.
4. **Compatible successor.** The successor's proven track record in the church, the affection of the people, and the ability to be a "DNA" carrier of the church's culture and vision. This does not and should not imply that the successor needs to be a younger clone of the outgoing pastor. But it does mean the successor should be able to lead with one foot in the past and the other firmly planted in the future. They must honor the culture but also be capable of changing it with wisdom where and when needed.
5. **Written plan.** A written plan that clearly outlines a process, roles, dates, and "triggers" that start the gradual transfer of authority in essential areas.
6. **Financial resources**. The church's fiscal health is needed to finance the transition from the planning stage to the one-year anniversary of the successor assuming full authority.

MAKING IT REAL
Prayer, Reflection, and Action Items

1. How does a church's governance structure influence the feasibility of implementing a mentored succession model?
2. Which of the four kinds of church governance models in this chapter resemble your church?
3. What challenges might your form of governance or bylaws present? What advantages do they offer?
4. What adjustments or customization might your church governance model require you to make to the seven stages of mentored succession mentioned in a previous chapter?
5. Jeff Harlow said he made a conscious decision to "make voting his friend." His approach involved congregational votes throughout the succession process. What are the benefits and potential pitfalls of using voting as a tool to gain ownership and measure buy-in for a new leader, as demonstrated by Jeff Harlow?
6. Mentored succession requires the total commitment of the outgoing pastor; otherwise, it will not be successful. What are three things you can do to ensure you can bring the following competencies to the table?

    - God's will. The outgoing pastor must be convinced that the transition is God's will for *everyone* involved and be willing to devote the time and effort needed to ensure its success.
    - Financial security. The outgoing pastor must have a financial plan to provide for their family without reliance upon the church.

- Marital unity. The outgoing pastor's spouse (and family) must fully support and help the successor succeed.
- Future ministry. The outgoing pastor must have clear direction on the next stage of ministry. In other words, they must have identified the next chapter of their ministry.
- Humility. The outgoing pastor must be prepared to meet the challenge with humility and see the church's success as more important than their own. Without humility on both sides of the equation, there will be no successful succession.

7. How can the church board actively support and participate in the succession planning process to ensure a smooth and successful transition, and what challenges might arise in achieving effective board involvement?
8. What strategies can be employed to evaluate and foster a culture of honor and respect between the outgoing pastor and the successor, and how can the successor be effectively prepared to honor the church's culture while guiding necessary changes?
9. How can the church develop a comprehensive written plan that details the succession process and ensures financial resources are in place, and what contingencies should be included to address potential challenges during the transition period?
10. How might you create an ongoing transition account to finance all future transitions? This account can be funded through personal donations from the pastor and board, modest monthly allocations from the church budget, and, at the appropriate time, congregation members after the plan is announced.

Family Members and Mentored Succession

Why are family members disproportionately chosen as successors? That was the question someone recently asked me as a transition specialist. Why? Many transition specialists, denominational leaders, and local churches are starting to question whether the traditional method of pastoral selection is effective. The model of bringing in outsiders with no understanding of the church's culture seems to be contributing to a cycle of short-term pastorates. Each cycle leaves the church a little weaker, smaller, and less focused than the one before. Transition experts Carolyn Weese and Russell Crabtree comment:

> *"The current model of pastoral transition, left over from a time when organizational learning was not as important, does not help congregations protect what is healthy and retain what they have learned."* [22]

Mentored succession usually involves the lead pastor and the board collaborating to select a person (current staff or future staff member) who is trained and mentored to one day lead the church. The goal is to identify a divinely called "DNA carrier" who understands the church, has proven themselves effective, is mentored by the outgoing pastor, and is trusted by the congregation. This model has become increasingly popular in the last five years. But have you noticed the seemingly disproportionate number of successors who are related to the outgoing pastor? Is this nepotism, or do family members make better successors?

First, let me say that, yes, there seems to be a disproportionate number of successors who are related to the outgoing pastor. The percentage is much higher in non-denominational and independent churches, where the lead pastor has more autonomy and less congregational involvement in decision-making. However, mentored succession is also gaining popularity in denominational churches with over 500 attendees, and family members are also becoming part of the succession plan there.

I was recently asked why I think this pattern exists. I would compare this reality to the role height plays in basketball. Not every great basketball player is tall, but height does create opportunities that a lack of it cannot. Let me suggest why qualified family members may have an advantage in the mentored succession journey.

1. **Calling**. Being related to the outgoing pastor is not enough when it comes to qualifying credentials. One must be qualified, competent, available, and willing. Pastoral leadership is not passed down like the crown of England. Nor is it the divine right of a lead pastor's family. But if a family member is indisputably called and anointed to lead, that mantle will be evident and confirmed long before a vacancy is considered. Like a sunrise, it becomes increasingly apparent to others over time.

2. **Commitment.** Family members who serve on staff are usually much more willing to sacrifice to see the church thrive. They often work harder, longer, and for less money because of their commitment to the church and loyalty to their family. They are more willing to accept long work schedules, intense project cycles, and less vacation time. They are also less likely to be tempted to seek employment elsewhere in difficult seasons. Numerous global studies in the corporate world mirror this reality. They show that well-run family companies are more profitable and generally last longer than other business types.[23] This is often because family work environments have a greater willingness to sacrifice, higher commitment levels, and longer vision trajectories. It is not that genetics make a person more devoted, but rather how the work environment and family relationships nurture a deeper sense of commitment.

3. **Teachability**. Family members tend to be more teachable and willing to put in the time to learn, ask questions, and receive honest feedback from a pastor to whom they are related. Because they are committed to each other in the long haul, they are more likely to have hard clarifying conversations without being offended or hurt enough to quit. Families know they have a life together outside the workplace. This makes them more willing to push through obstacles and learn from each other.

4. **Stewardship.** Family members seem to take their role more seriously as stewards of the church. Like puzzle pieces, they realize they are one small piece of the church's history. However, exterior candidates can be a little more self-centric in not taking the time to learn and appreciate the history or culture of the church. They may also see the church's genesis as the moment they arrived. While some staff are quick to run during a crisis, family members often see the church as an entrustment needing perseverance, resiliency, and stewardship.

5. **DNA carriers.** When doing an organ transplant, doctors look first to family donors who share the same genes. Why? Because they already possess the same DNA—a molecule in the body that carries all the genetic information about a person. When it comes to culture, qualified family members can be organizational DNA carriers

who can more easily translate and transfer the church's vision, values, and ethos. Family members often have two powerful forces driving them. First, they already know the culture of the church, city, and immediate community. Secondly, they can immediately understand the "why" behind the church's past, present, and future.

6. **Legacy**. Qualified family members often personalize their concept of legacy. They are more motivated to rise above obstacles because they want to honor their family name and legacy of ministry. They feel a sense of obligation to those who have gone before them and those who will follow behind them. This can give them greater resiliency, endurance, and long-term commitment to seeing the church succeed.

7. **Honor.** Because family relationships involve an underlying culture of honor, successors who are related to the lead pastor are more willing to be patient and wait for the right time for the transition. However, one of the common obstacles to mentored succession is the impatience of the successor. Once they are chosen, a successor can become impatient, rushed, and even push for timelines to move faster than is wise. Mentored succession can expose our deepest insecurities and the worst version of ourselves. That is true of both the outgoing pastor and the successor. Author Scott

Wilson claims a culture of honor and help from a third party enabled him and his father to navigate many obstacles. "I was certain God called me to transition with my father. Honor helped me be patient and serve him and the vision while waiting for the right time," said Wilson.[24] Ecclesiastes 3:1 teaches us the importance of patience, saying, *"There is a time for everything, and a season for every activity under the heavens."* The culture of honor, trust, and respect among family members often holds the dark side of insecurity at bay long enough to intersect with God's timing. That sense of honor ends up working double duty because it goes both ways.

It should be noted that both church and corporate history are stained by the failure of family leadership legacies gone wrong. Leadership and succession consultant Sam Chand acknowledges that family succession has its own set of obstacles. These include unreasonable assumptions, familiarity, entitlement, dishonor, and parental interference. "I'm all for family successors as long as the successor is qualified," says Chand.[25]

So, back to the question. Why are family successors more common in the succession equation? The answer is that family members do not inherently make better successors but can have an advantage that makes them a better fit. The only time a family member should be chosen is when God calls and anoints them to this task, and that anointing is confirmed by the church's leadership community and congregation.

MAKING IT REAL
Prayer, Reflection, and Action Items

1. Why are family members often seen as disproportionately represented in mentored succession models?
2. How does a congregation's front row seat to the development of a young person's calling influence the selection of a family member as a pastoral successor?
3. In what ways does commitment from family members differ from that of external candidates when serving a church?
4. How might family members' ministerial teachability benefit a church during a pastoral transition?
5. Why might family members take a more serious role in the stewardship of a church compared to external successors?
6. What does it mean for a family member to be a "DNA carrier" of a church, and how might this benefit the congregation?
7. How does the concept of legacy motivate family members to persist through obstacles in pastoral leadership?
8. In what ways does a culture of honor contribute to the success of a mentored family succession?
9. What are some potential dangers or obstacles that can arise from family leadership legacies, according to Sam Chand?

10. How can the church ensure that a family member is truly called and anointed to lead, rather than simply being chosen due to their relationship with the outgoing pastor?

Pros and Cons of Professional Search Firms

The pastoral search process has been monetized over the last few years, and some churches are considering hiring a search firm or "headhunters" to find candidates. While paying someone else to shoulder this difficult task may seem inviting and beneficial, allow me to present a few advantages to leading the search yourself and using advisors to help you along the way. I'll then conclude by highlighting why a professional search firm may be the right choice to help you identify a potential successor.

Advantages of Self-Led Searches

Organizational learning. Hiring a search team deprives your church of the opportunity to develop organizational skills it will undoubtedly need in the future. The average church experiences a pastoral transition once every 5-8 years. That means there will be a time when your church will need these core competencies. There may even be a transition when the church cannot afford the high cost of search firms. Developing the skills and organizational memory to navigate these waters now will develop leaders, increase faith, mature commitment, and set your church up to face future challenges. It will also give your people more confidence in the process.

Increased resiliency. Easy is not always the best way, and shortcuts can be overrated. As a matter of fact, God led the children of Israel the long way to the Promised Land to give them time to develop skills that the future would require. The scriptures tell us, *"When Pharaoh let the people go, God did not lead them on the road through the Philistine country, though that was shorter. For God said, 'If they face war, they might change their minds and return to Egypt.' So God led the people around by the desert road toward the Red Sea. The Israelites went up out of Egypt armed for battle."* (Exodus 13:17-18)

Unbiased process. Many search firms gain income from two sources: churches needing a pastor and pastors needing career consulting. In some cases, there is a conflict of interest that needs to be addressed because search firms often recommend to client churches people they are also consulting or who they have met in prior cases. Another reality is that search firms usually work on a commission basis, which means the higher the salary offered the higher their cost to you will be. This could lead to a conflict of interest whereby they are not necessarily communicating what is best for the church but what would benefit them. It is also possible that their potential income from you is not enough to ensure your search is a high priority for them. Other firms also have minimum time periods outlined in their consulting contract. I know one firm that requires two years of fees in return for helping churches find a successor. The contract's first year identifies a successor, and the second year coaches that person after they assume leadership. That ends up being a serious bill and legislates a coaching relationship the new pastor may not appreciate. You will need to ensure that an agreement does not involve unwanted baggage.

Maximized access. Hiring a search firm places another person between you and prospective candidates. Because search firms mediate compatibility, there is always one person guiding, screening, vetting, interacting, speaking on your behalf, negotiating salaries, and filtering information.

Increased expenses. Search firms are expensive and usually charge a church 35-40% of the church's total remuneration package for the lead pastor. For example, if your salary, health benefits, housing, and other remuneration for the lead pastor total $70,000, they will charge your church between $26,250 and $28,000 for their services. Others charge a monthly fee that is usually between $4,000 - $6,000 for the search duration. In addition to this hefty fee, you will still pay all the other normal expenses associated with the transition, such as interviewing, travel, candidating, and relocating a pastor. As mentioned earlier, this excludes additional fees that may be contracted for post-transition coaching.

Focused faith. Author Richard Blackaby cautions churches considering a search firm against transferring their faith in God to faith in man. Blackaby warns, "Take time to examine your approach. Is it biblical? Is it God honoring? Does it force you to rely on God or a consultant?"[26] The Old Testament records several instances where God warned His people about developing an unhealthy dependence on treaties, wealth, war horses, kings, and other inferior places to deposit one's trust. Blackaby's warning is warranted.

Advantages of Professional Search Firms

However, there are situations in which a church should consider hiring a search firm to give advice and help find a successor for several key reasons.

Experience. Search firms specialize in ministerial recruitment and have experience identifying candidates that fit the church's specific spiritual, cultural, gift mix, and leadership needs. Some may even have a track record for identifying and profiling potential DNA carriers.

Broader candidate pool. A ministerial search firm may have access to a more extensive network of potential candidates. They can often reach beyond the local community, state, or geographical region to help the church identify more leadership options to explore.

Efficient process. Identifying a successor can be lengthy and complex. A ministerial search firm may be structured to handle much of the administrative burden, allowing the church to focus on maintaining viable ministry while search-related tasks are subcontracted.

Objective screening. Professional search firms may be able to offer a more objective, third-party perspective and evaluation process that helps prevent biases from influencing the selection process.

Confidentiality. If the current pastor is retiring or planning a scheduled exit and the church wants to approach currently employed candidates, search firms may be more capable of maintaining discretion and confidentiality throughout the process.

Organizational fit. A search firm can help ensure a potential successor matches the church's theology, mission, and values, making it more likely that the new pastor will integrate well with the congregation, its lay leadership team, and staff.

Some of the most popular search firms are...
- Vanderbloem Search Group, https://www.vanderbloemen.com
- Slingshot Group, https://slingshotgroup.org

- Agora Search Group, https://www.agorasearchgroup.com
- The Shepherd's Staff, https://theshepherdsstaff.com
- Expand Consulting Partners, www.expandconsultingpartners.com

MAKING IT REAL
Prayer, Reflection, and Action Items

1. What are some potential drawbacks of hiring a search firm for a pastoral search process?
2. How does leading a pastoral search internally benefit the church's organizational learning?
3. How can a church avoid conflicts of interest when hiring a search firm?
4. What are the financial implications of hiring a professional search firm, and how might they affect a church's budget?
5. How does hiring a search firm place limitations on direct access between the church and prospective candidates?
6. How might reliance on search firms conflict with the need for a church to place faith in God during a pastoral search process?
7. What advantages do search firms offer regarding their experience with ministerial recruitment?
8. In what ways can a professional search firm access a broader pool of candidates compared to a self-led search?
9. How might the administrative burden of a pastoral search be alleviated by hiring a professional search firm?
10. How could the confidentiality provided by a search firm be important for certain churches, especially regarding candidates currently employed elsewhere?

Standout Literature

Of all the material I have read on mentored succession, I have found the following to be standout resources.

1. **Lee Kricher's book**, *Seamless Pastoral Transition, 3 Imperatives – 6 Pitfalls*, is an excellent work focused on the leadership an outgoing pastor must give to mentored succession. His transparency and practical examples from his own journey are thought provoking.[27]
2. **Will Heath's book**, *Embracing Succession, Helping Ministry Leaders Confront the Personal Side of Transition*, is a must-read for any minister considering retirement and succession planning.
3. **Gary Smith's book,** *Pastoral Transitions, A Seamless Handoff of Leadership*, may be the best resource on the practical, emotional, and spiritual maturity that will be required of the outgoing pastor.[28] It is a must-read for any minister transitioning out after a long pastorate.

4. **Glen Wolf** is one of the first millennials to make an academic and thoughtful contribution to this body of work. Glen earned a doctorate in the subject and his thesis is an outstanding read that maintains a wonderful balance between academic study and practical application. Chapter five recommends a list of things both the outgoing and incoming pastor must do to contribute to a successful succession. The entire work is outstanding, but chapter five alone is gold.[29]
5. **Tom Mullins'** book, *Passing the Leadership Baton: A Winning Transition Plan for Your Ministry*, is one of the finest books I have read concerning strategic succession.[30] Mullins is the founding pastor who led Christ Fellowship Church, a nondenominational, multisite church with more than 20,000 members. He and his board collaborated in one of the most successful planned successions in megachurch history. Although his book focuses on the mentored succession model, it is filled with seasoned, and practical advice for pastors, boards, and successors.
6. **Jeff Harlow's** book, *Dancing with Cinderella: Leading a Healthy Church Transition,* outlines the wise integration of the mentored succession plan while being true to the congregational/presbyterian model of church governance.[31] His book is a practical and transparent example of how a strong leader can transition a church without being autocratic.

7. **Terry Roberts'** book, *Passing the Baton: Planning for Pastoral Transition*, gives an excellent perspective of the mentored success model from an Assemblies of God perspective. Roberts gives practical advice and examples of AG churches that have successfully used this model.[32]
8. **Gary L. Johnson's** book, *Leader Shift: One Becomes Less While Another Becomes More,* offers several convincing arguments for this model.[33] Johnson gives some of the best scriptural applications as well as good and bad examples of mentored succession in leading corporations. He recognizes that each plan must be tailor-made for the church while outlining essential pieces that must be present in all applications.
9. **Bob Russell's** 2010 groundbreaking book, *Transition Plan: 7 Secrets Every Leader Needs to Know*, was among the first to highlight the success of the mentored succession plan.[34] Russell served as the lead minister of Southeast Christian Church in Louisville, Kentucky, for 40 years until he retired in 2006. It is a large church with more than 26,000 members. Amazingly, years after leaving, his transition plan has resulted in continued growth. The outline of Russell's plan has become a template for organizations of all kinds.
10. **Barna Group's** 2019 study entitled, *Leadership Transitions: How Churches Navigate Pastoral Change and Stay Healthy*, offered the following five goals for outgoing leaders:[35]
    - Communicate clearly, honestly, and often.

- Target unity. Remember, it's about the Kingdom.
- If you can, plan! Don't coast out, but leave with intentionality.
- Aim for a graceful exit. Make a hard thing easy for others.
- Keep asking why. Be aware of your emotions, motives, and insecurities.

11. **Dr. Jerry David's** book, *Honorable Design: The Art and Order of Generational Transition*, is unique in addressing the need for a culture of honor and how the outgoing pastor must take the lead in creating this needed culture.[36]

12. **Expand Consulting Partners'** book entitled, *Tsunami, Open Secrets to Pastoral Succession & Transition* is more of an introduction to their paid consulting services and philosophy than a how-to resource. However, the book's three appendixes offer outstanding questions and checklists to help identify the needs and expectations of the outgoing and incoming pastors.[37]

Want to Learn More?

Want access to more resources on pastoral transition and succession? Here is a list of Gene Roncone's resources on this critical topic.

- *Pastoral Search Consulting by Gene Roncone.* Hire Gene to partner with your team to provide pastoral and mentored succession coaching.
- *Rise Up, Pastoral Transition Reference Manual,* the most comprehensive, researched, and practical reference for pastoral transitions and succession planning available today.
- *Rise Up Podcast.* Audio coaching for search committees concerning topics related to pastoral transition and succession.
- *Defying Gravity, How to Thrive in a Pastoral Transition.* Finally, a short paperback book for everyday church folks on how to survive and thrive in a pastoral transition. Available in English and Spanish.
- *Defying Gravity Small Group Curriculum.* An interactive small group curriculum to empower

ordinary church people to make a positive contribution to the transition journey.
- *360° Prayer Guide.* A spiritual covering for every stage and person involved in your pastoral transition.
- *Refreshed Devotional.* An online well of encouragement for search teams.
- *Female Lead Pastors: A Discussion Worth Having.* A collaborative resource by over 25 district/network superintendents to help your pastoral search team consider the issues surrounding female leadership.
- *10 Mistakes Pastoral Search Committees Make.* A PDF resource by Gene Roncone.

Check out www.generoncone.org/riseup.

End Notes

[1] Bob Russel and Bryan Bucher, *Transition Plan—7 Secrets Every Leader Needs to Know,* Ministers Label Publishing, Louisville, KY, 2010, p. 18.

[2] William Vanderbloemen and Warren Bird, *Next: Pastoral Succession That Works,* Baker Books, Grand Rapids, 2015, p. 57.

[3] Carolyn Weese and J. Russell Crabtree, *The Elephant in the Boardroom: Speaking the Unspoken About Pastoral Transitions,* Jossey-Bass Publishers, Hoboken, NY, 2004, p. 26.

[4] Gary Smith, *Pastoral Transitions, A Seamless Handoff of Leadership,* EnGedi Publishing, Corpus Christi, TX, 2022, p. 41.

[5] Jerry David, *Honorable Design: The Art and Order of Generational Transition,* Brookstone Publishing Group, 2019, p. 6.

[6] Andrew Flowers, *Leading Through Succession: Why Pastoral Leadership Is Key to a Healthy Transition,* Published by Andrew Flowers, 2017, pp. 6, 8.

[7] Carolyn Weese and J. Russell Crabtree, *The Elephant in the Boardroom: Speaking the Unspoken About Pastoral Transitions,* Jossey-Bass Publishers, Hoboken, NJ, 2004.

[8] Gary L. Johnson, *Leader Shift: One Becomes Less While Another Becomes More,* 2013, Published by Gary L. Johnson, Foreword.

[9] Terry Roberts, *Passing the Baton: Planning for Pastoral Transition*, Published by Terry Roberts, 2015, p. 7.

[10] Barna Group, *Leadership Transitions: How Churches Navigate Pastoral Change and Stay Healthy*, Barna Group, PDF, 2019, p. 17.

[11] Terry Roberts, *Passing the Baton: Planning for Pastoral Transition*, Published by Terry Roberts, 2015, pp. 27-36.

[12] Glen Wolf, (2020). *A Strategic Plan to Assist Pastors in the Succession Between a Mentoring Lead Pastor and His or Her Mentee*, [Doctor of Ministry, DMin], Southwestern University, pp. 1-4.

[13] Bryant Wright, *Succession, Preparing Your Ministry for the Next Leader*, B&H Publishing Group, Nashville, Tennessee, 2022, p. 22.

[14] Glen Wolf, (2020). *A Strategic Plan to Assist Pastors in the Succession Between a Mentoring Lead Pastor and His or Her Mentee*, [Doctor of Ministry, DMin], Southwestern University, p. 63.

[15] Bishop Walter Harvey, *Alley-Oop, Keys to Pastoral Succession*, Walter Harvey Ministries, 2021.

[16] Will Heath, *Embracing Succession, Helping Ministry Leaders Confront the Personal Side of Transition*, CrossLink Publishing, Rapid City, South Dakota, 2020, pp. 64-65.

[17] William Vanderbloemen and Warren Bird, *Next: Pastoral Succession That Works*, Baker Books, Grand Rapids, 2020, p. 31.

[18] Frank Damazio, *The Vanguard Leader: A New Breed of Leader to Encounter the Future*, Bible Temple Publishing, Portland, OR, 1994, p. 309.

[19] Jeff Harlow, *Dancing with Cinderella: Leading a Healthy Church Transition*, Epiphany Publishing, Indianapolis, IN, 2017, p. 68.

[20] Barna Group, *Leadership Transitions: How Churches Navigate Pastoral Change and Stay Healthy*, Barna Group, PDF, 2019, p. 24.

[21] Gary Smith, *Pastoral Transitions, A Seamless Handoff of Leadership*, EnGedi Publishing, Corpus Christi, TX, pp. 17-23.

[22] Carolyn Weese and J. Russell Crabtree, *The Elephant in the Boardroom: Speaking the Unspoken About Pastoral Transitions,* Jossey-Bass Publishers, Hoboken, NJ, 2004, p. 179.

[23] Boldentity, August 14, 2018, *Managing Family Business Challenges: How Family Businesses Succeed According to Experts*, https://boldentity.com/how-family-businesses-succeed-according-to-experts/

[24] Conversation with Scott Wilson on October 21, 2022.

[25] October 20, 2022, texting thread between Gene Roncone and Samuel Chand.

[26] Richard Blackaby, *Your Next Pastor, A God-Centered Guide for Pastor Search Committees*, Blackaby Ministries International, Jonesboro, GA 30237, 2022, p. 7.

[27] Lee Kricher, *Seamless Pastoral Transitions, 3 Imperatives – 6 Pitfalls*, Xulon Press, Maitland, FL, 2022, pp. 49-55 and 73-82.

[28] Gary Smith, *Pastoral Transitions, A Seamless Handoff of Leadership*, EnGedi Publishing, Corpus Christi, TX, 2020.

[29] Glen Wolf, (2020). *A Strategic Plan to Assist Pastors in the Succession Between a Mentoring Lead Pastor and His or Her Mentee*, [Doctor of Ministry, DMin], Southwestern University.

[30] Tom Mullins, *Passing the Leadership Baton: A Winning Transition Plan for Your Ministry*, Thomas Nelson, Nashville, TN, 2015. Mullins and his board were wise enough to recognize that a seasoned and proven staff member had a better chance at succeeding him than a promising outsider. Mullins selected a successor and then systematically and strategically mentored him until he retired. The church continued growing through the transition.

[31] Jeff Harlow, *Dancing with Cinderella: Leading a Healthy Church Transition*, Epiphany Publishing, Indianapolis, IN, 2017.

[32] Terry Roberts, *Passing the Baton: Planning for Pastoral Transition*, Published by Terry Roberts, 2015.

[33] Gary L Johnson, *Leader Shift, One Becomes Less While Another Becomes More,* Moeller Printing, Inc., Indianapolis, IN, January 2013.

[34] Bob Russell, *Transition Plan: 7 Secrets Every Leader Needs to Know*, Ministers Label Publishing; 1st edition, 2010.

[35] Barna Group, *Leadership Transitions: How Churches Navigate Pastoral Change and Stay Healthy*, Barna Group, PDF, 2019, pp. 95-101.

[36] Jerry David, *Honorable Design: The Art and Order of Generational Transition*, Brookstone Publishing Group, 2019.

[37] Expand Consulting Partners, *Tsunami, Open Secrets to Pastoral Succession & Transition*, Expand Publishing, 2022.

Made in the USA
Columbia, SC
23 September 2024